RUBY
WARRIORS

RUBY WARRIORS

Saving Arth

JEYA CARMICHAEL

ISBN. 979-8-89109-339-3 (paperback)
ISDN. 979-8-89109-340-9 (ebook)

Thanks to my husband for his support and understanding when I am cocooned in my writing!

CONTENTS

CHAPTER 1

What Are We Doing in a Parallel World?

S tep into the world of Aurora Priya Banks, Lizzy Devi Samuels, and Lance Sanjay Tully-three inseparable eleven-year-olds who share an unbreakable bond of friendship. Nestled in the picturesque town of Las Palomas, near the mesmerizing White Sands of New Mexico this trio of adventurers finds joy in the simplest of things. One thing they absolutely adore is their tradition of sleepovers, a cherished ritual that brings them even closer.

As the stars aligned it was Aurora's turn to play host for their latest sleepover escapade. Eager to embark on another unforgettable adventure the trio made their way to the trusty shed that housed their well-loved camping gear. With each item they retrieved memories of the past weekend of camping trips flooded their minds. A testament to the countless explorations and laughter they had shared.

With a shared sense of adventure and camaraderie, the trio set up their camping gear. Lance took charge of assembling the pop-up tent, capably unfolding, and securing its poles to create a cozy shelter for the night. Aurora handed out the lanterns, making sure they had fresh batteries, which created a warm glow around their camp. As they worked together, their laughter filled the air, blending with the sounds of nature and the rustling of leaves.

As the campfire crackled, the cool night embraced Aurora, Lizzy, and Lance. They sat together chatting and exchanging stories. They were blissfully unaware of the magical moments that awaited them.

The next morning, they hurriedly ate their breakfast and set off to the flea market with their moms. Dads were off doing what dads do best—playing golf.

The friends didn't realize that they were about to embark on a journey that would change their lives forever. Aurora, Lizzy, and Lance are about to save the world and they don't know it yet. It's such a huge ask to put on the shoulders of eleven-year-olds. If they fail to achieve their quest, they may never see their parents, family, and friends.

At the flea market, Aurora noticed a gem and rock store.

"Hey guys, let's go in here to see what we can get," Aurora shouted, running toward the store.

The store was full of colorful rocks, beads, and gems of all different hues.

Their jaws dropped as they stood there, completely mesmerized by the sheer opulence of all the gorgeous, shiny things in the store. It was a sight that left them speechless and filled with awe and wonder.

"Wow!" they all say in unison.

The woman, who was reminiscent of a gypsy, waved them over with her open hand. She had long silver hair and hoop earrings that glinted in the light.

The three of them carefully went around everything in the store to get to her.

"Welcome my dears!" she cooed. "I have a special bargain gem, and I only have three left. You three look like incredibly special friends. Three shiny rubies for three bright best friends,"

"Wow, it looks impressive and shiny. It also looks very spendy," Lizzy commented.

"Don't worry, my dear; just put it on. Come here, darlings, and I'll put them on each of you, and you can look in the mirror and see their beauty."

She put the shiny ruby pendant on a leather string and placed one on each of them.

"Wow, look at the pendant shimmer and glow. It's as if the sun shines through it," Lance exclaimed, adjusting his hair, and admiring it.

"It is a gorgeous ruby, but it looks spendy. We can't afford this," remarked Aurora.

"Darlings, darlings, they are beautiful on you. It's as if you're chosen to wear them. The cost is only five dollars each."

"Only five dollars! Wow, what a bargain." Lance replied.

"Darlings, I told you, no? You three will love it."

They paid the kindly middle-aged lady, and as they were leaving the store—Swoosh! They were teleported to a new place.

"What—What just happened?" Aurora asked.

The look on their faces was priceless! With enormous round eyes and eyebrows lifted, they took the scene in.

"Didn't see that coming!" Lizzy giggled.

"Don't be afraid. Welcome to Arth, a parallel world to your earth. I am Daisy Duggan,"

"Welcome. I am Choxie McKenzie." said, curtsying.

"They look lovely fluttering in the air like hummingbirds," Lizzy remarked, amazed.

Looking around, they marveled at the painted murals and statues of Indian Kings. The beautiful, raised fonts told their stories. Ivy plants wrapped around the palace columns in a candy cane pattern. Beautiful climbing and fragrant jasmine plants attract hummingbirds zooming in and out of the vines. Their fluttering wings and pointed beaks headed to the sweet nectar of the jasmine flowers to feed.

The huge grassy manicured garden had a sizable pond with lily pads and reeds growing on the edges of it along with a variety of wildflowers in vivid colors, including orchids, tiger lilies, violets, and daisies. A cluster of beautiful, colorful butterflies, bees, and dragonflies swarmed around the flowers swaying in the breeze. They couldn't get over the gorgeous colors and hues of the rainbow in the garden.

The three turned to see an enormous lake with mother ducks and ducklings quacking up a storm and large fish jumping up in the air. Above the lake was a five-story tall, wide building floating in the air with a huge propeller spinning in the back. People were riding harnessed ostriches in the air. Dwarfs, elves, and trolls rode in a large prairie wagon hitched to six flamingoes flapping their beautiful, pink, and white wings.

Lizzy exclaimed, "I've seen it all now!"

After they drank in the beautiful scenery, the fairies escorted them to see the King.

"Please follow us, our King, Raja Vijay, anxiously awaits to meet you," Daisy said.

CHAPTER 2

The Truth Becomes Known.

"Your Highness," Daisy and Choxi say with palms together and a nod of their heads, "Your visitors have arrived."

"My dears, you have grown so much. The last time I saw you, you children were babies. I see that your parents have raised you well." King Vijay continued, "I am deeply sorry that I must reveal some truths to you so that you all can do what you must do."

The three friends looked at each other with one eyebrow lifted, and lips tight and closed.

Aurora, Lizzy, and Lance followed Daisy and Choxi's actions and put their palms together and nodded their heads.

"Come, come, come, and sit down. You're going to want to sit down, trust me, my dears. Choxi, please have Nesam bring the children a cold drink and some strawberry ice cream."

"Yum! My favorite," Lance said, rubbing his tummy.

Nesam, The Royal Chef, returned with a tray of strawberry ice cream and water. The children didn't want anything but water to drink since they had ice cream.

"Nesan is our Royal Chef children and if you want something to eat or drink, please go see Nesam." King Vijay said.

"Hi Nesam!" The three of them said and waved their hand.

"Hello, your highnesses!" Responded Nesam.

Nesam was a beautiful lady with a short stature and long plaited hair. She ran the king's palace smoothly and she was loved by all because of her kindness. Nesam was happy because finally there were children at the palace, and she loved children.

"Jeepers, Your Highness, why are we here?" asked Lizzy.

"Man-oh-man, this ice cream is out of this world!" Lance exclaimed.

"We are out of our world, Lance, duh!" remarked Lizzy, rolling her eyes.

"Oh Man, yeah." And they all laughed.

"You have an exquisite palace, Your Highness."

"Thank you, my dear Aurora. My ancestors built this palace in one thousand AD. The first King was King Ashok. My line descends from him. Since that time, every King has added something to the palace. In the beginning, the palace was quite small. As the palace families grew, they added many rooms and spaces for living and maids' quarters. Queen Shanti and I have added ten suites, or independent living quarters, with their own rooms—living rooms, dining rooms, and kitchens. These suites are facing the great Lake of Devi Krishna, a beautiful view."

The King took a drink of hot tea. "We built the suites hoping that one day our children would come home with their families and live in the palace and have their own space. The Kings before me created beautiful gardens, and we added to that. We added more fruit trees, shade trees, and flowers of all wonderful colors. My beautiful wife had the trellis of jasmine done. It also gives us shade and privacy when we sit and take our tea in the mornings." The King took another drink of tea.

"Excuse me, Your Highness, what truths do you want to reveal to us?" asked Aurora.

"Yes, my dear, I just got carried away telling you the history of the palace. We on Arth need your help. Long ago, it was predicted that three royal cousins will be born of three princesses. They will have special powers to save Arth and Earth, according to Deva Krishna, meaning Son of the gods. He told us about the future and what we should do, in the Big Book of Deva Krishna."

The king continued, "There was a time of famine during the solar flare. The heat was so unbearable that people had to take shelter in caves, in underground bunkers, and in space. Our crops didn't produce the foods we needed. Unfortunately, there was such a severe lack of food, it even resulted in some people dying and some being maimed. During that period, a team of scientists conducted research on the possibility of life on a smaller planet within our galaxy while in space. They unexpectedly discovered a planet that we now refer to as Prodigy. We named it Prodigy because it resembles Arth's atmosphere, and its soil was ideal for planting."

The king paused to reflect. "A significant number of people from Arth departed on shuttles to move to Prodigy. My parents, The King and Queen, moved to Earth to live. Others built underground shelters and stayed. Many died because they couldn't find shelter and food. We were just young children. Thirty years had passed before we moved back to Arth to settle down. Both my parents felt so fortunate to return to Arth. When they passed, we buried them in the place where they rightfully belong."

"Okay, but why have you summoned us, Your Highness?" asked.

"My dear ones, the three cousins are the three of you! You were born to three royal princesses, your mothers."

"What?" shouted Aurora.

"Is this for real?" Lizzy shouted, too.

"Man, oh man, I don't believe what I'm hearing," Lance spoke out. "Does that mean that you are our grandpa?"

"Yes, my son, I am your grandpa."

"Uh, what do we call you then?" asked Lizzy.

"You may call me Grandpa."

"So, what is the problem, Your Highness, I mean Grandpa?" asked Aurora.

"I have a brother named Raju who has always held a grudge against me for becoming king after our father's passing. Despite being second in line to the throne, he could not come to terms with his place in the royal family. Raju represented Arth in other nations. Our capital is Nadu, Bangla. My brother served as a representative, he and his wife became space marauders because they weren't satisfied with our royal system, which according to him did not treat them fairly. Now that he has all the recruits he needs, he has come back to steal water, diamonds, obsidian, and food. We need the three of you to send them back to space and release our people."

"Grandpa, we're going to need someone to help us identify our powers and how to use them," Lizzy pointed out.

"Yes, yes, your powers were bound when you lived on Earth. The ruby around your neck has removed the ties that bound you. Tomorrow morning, you will meet Anthony and his wife Victoria; they will teach and guide you about the magical powers you have."

CHAPTER 3

Preparing to Fight for Earth and Arth

"Good morning, Your Highnesses. My name is Anthony, and my wife's name is Victoria."

Aurora warmly greeted them, "Good morning, Anthony and Victoria."

Aurora looked lovely in a black blouse with beautiful blue floral prints that reach her elbows. She smartly tucked it into her jeans.

"Good morning!" greeted Lizzy with a cheerful twirl of her hair and a carefree dance. Her beautiful brown hair with golden flecks was in a ponytail tied up with a checkered red ribbon that matched her button-down red and white checkered shirt and jeans.

"Put it here, man!" Lance extended his hand.

Usually preferring T-shirts and cargo shorts, Lance decided to wear a beige polo shirt and jeans. The blond highlights in his light brown hair added to his charm. The girls were aware of his keen interest in learning about animals and bugs.

Anthony and Victoria shook Lance's outstretched hand. "Your Great-great-great-great-grandmother was an elf from Athenea, Alvania," Anthony started. "Your magic comes from her elfin bloodline. That's why elves will always protect all your bloodlines. Now, Victoria will do some magical exercises to evaluate your magical abilities."

"First, I want to see what powers you have, so listen carefully and do exactly what I say," Victoria instructed. "All right, I want you to put your arms out with palms up."

"Aurora, and Lance, I can see that you have the power to throw flames. You must be ready to use it to protect each other. Put your palms together to extinguish the flames. Good."

"Okay Lizzy, swipe your hand from left to right."

"Oh my gosh! I am an ice queen! I can freeze things." Lizzy said excitedly. "Can I freeze people?"

"Yes, but you must be very careful that you turn them back within seventy-two hours, or they will die," Victoria said.

"Oh no, I hope I never have to do that."

"Okay, arms out with palms facing forward, and say 'shield,'" Victoria said to the children. "Okay, I can see that all three of you have the power to protect yourselves. This will protect you from weapons, fireballs, and anything else you need protection from. Your shield will also protect you from animals and creatures on your journey. You can teleport and move around safely with your shields up."

"Please turn around. Do you see the statue of the Lord Krishna behind you? I would like the three of you to teleport to the X near the statue. Think about your desired destination and teleport there. Do you have questions? All right, you may teleport whenever you feel ready.

They all nod their heads.

"Oh dear, where is Lance? Hmm . . . I expected this to happen. I know where Lance may be. Stay here and I'll go see and bring him back if he is there." And off Victoria went.

Victoria teleported to Krishna's temple and found Lance looking around, confused.

"I'm lost and didn't know how to get back," Lance said sheepishly.

"Let's go back and we'll talk about that. Now focus on getting to point X."

They both got back to Aurora and Lizzy.

"Lance, where were you? We were worried about you," said Lizzy.

"This is what I was afraid of. Be specific with each other as to the exact destination you all want to teleport. You can make your own mark as a destination point."

"Like you marked the X by the Krishna statue?" asked Aurora.

"Yes, Aurora. It can be a simple mark made in the dirt with a stick, or a pile of stones to mark the destination—if it is outdoors with nothing close by," Victoria replied. "I will give each of you a small pouch of the dust from the Unicorn's horns. This dust will put beings to sleep, and it is used to erase memories."

Continuing, Victoria instructed, "After lunch, I will take you one at a time for thirty minutes to figure out what your other hidden abilities are."

Anthony asked, "So, did you all learn what you needed to know from Victoria? She is the most intelligent magical creature. By the way, your grandmother will see us for dinner tonight. When she sees all three of you, she will be absolutely thrilled."

Lizzy, Lance, and Aurora looked forward to meeting Grandma! With wide grins on their faces, they held hands and danced in a circle.

Nesam entered, announcing, "Your Highnesses, lunch is served. Today, we are serving roasted chicken, asparagus, chicken rice, and fresh cucumbers. For a refreshing cold drink, we have mango smoothies."

"Thank-you Nesam." King Vijay says.

CHAPTER 4

Their Journey through the Elfin and Troll Region

They hiked to the region where the Marauders used the elves of Elvin and the trolls from the region of Gordo near Elvin. Elvin villages are all around the mountaintop. The Elvin King lives at the very top in his ornate castle, and the Troll homes are hidden among the vegetation. After a day and night of hiking, they arrived in Gordo. The villagers were very welcoming and looking forward to meeting them.

"Welcome to Troll Valley!" shouted the villagers. They served them food and drinks, and everyone ate by the light of the bonfire. The villagers chatted about what had happened to their loved ones in the village.

"I'm Doria. Those evil Marauders took my husband and son. They need the men to mine obsidian to make weapons."

"I'm Marla, and the Marauders captured my husband, Monahan. My husband is a good cook. While our men are away, we have had to work in the fields and take care of the home and children."

The visitors listened to the villagers and ate. They asked them if they knew any of their weaknesses.

"Grandpa Finn, come here. You're the oldest and know so much about the Marauders. Grandpa Finn is an elder in our village and knows this story well. His parents told him the story of how their world will be saved by the children of three princesses." Doria explained.

They listen intently to Grandpa Choxie. The young children of the village heard this story for the first time, as Doria did.

"Many centuries ago, Arth suffered from famine and Mother Nature's wrath. The earth was thrown into an ice age that destroyed everything, yet it also created a new earth where living things could survive. Mars had shifted away from the sun, so people survived there. They built a huge biodome with cities and homes. Then we had visitors who came from Mars to kidnap our people and take them away to build their biodome. Our ancestors told us the story of the people who ran away to live on Mars. The ones who remained behind survived under the most aggressive conditions of weather and people. Many people lost their humanity and did many evil things to humankind and other new cultures of magical beings."

Grandpa Choxie drew a deep breath and continued, "So now these Marauders come to steal food, kidnap people, and steal diamonds and obsidian from our mines. The wormhole only opens once every seven years and then for only two weeks. They have from the time they arrive before the wormhole closes to get back to Mars or Prodigy. However, we have seventy-two hours to get rid of the Marauders by closing the wormhole for another seven years. They have about three days left now."

"Your great-great-great-great-grandmother was a powerful good elf," he continued. "Rubies bring special powers to the true descendants of Queen Sophia. They strengthen your powers. It's written in all our books that the royal grandchildren would save Arth. And as a result, they would save Earth."

"Goodnight," the three said as they bedded down for the night in a tent that was warm and cozy.

Their great-great-great-great-grandmother Sofia suddenly woke the three royals up.

"Hello, my darlings, I'm your Grandma Sophia."

"Grandma Sophia, but you're dead!" Lance blurted out.

"Yes, Lance I am," chuckled Grandma Sophia. "But I can show myself to you because of magic," she explained, sitting in a red, comfy royal Queen's chair.

"Come my dears, would you like some hot chocolate?"

"Yes, please," they all said.

A female maid made hot chocolate in what looked like a kitchen in their tent. They looked surprised at how amazing their tent looked.

The maid served them their hot chocolates, and they sat closer to the Queen on beautiful ornate chairs with overstuffed soft cushions.

"Wow," mouthed Lizzy to her cousins. Awestruck, they admired the richness and beauty of the tent.

"I came to let you know this journey is going to get more treacherous. You must keep your guard up and be aware of your surroundings. Just know that I have friends in the Arachne Forest to help if you need it," Grandma Sophia warned.

CHAPTER 5

Fear in the Arachne Forest

The trio and a dozen of King Raja's soldiers woke up early and ate breakfast with the trolls and elves. They ate pancakes with homemade blueberry syrup and topped with fresh blueberries.

"Umm . . ., this smells so delicious," said Aurora.

"Yes!" agreed Lizzy, cutting into the pancakes.

Lance was already eating the pancakes.

After breakfast, they left for Arachne Forest; it took half a day to walk there. They arrived there about noonish and stopped to eat and fuel their bodies.

"It's time to cross the Arachne Forest," Lance announced. "Look at all the trees swaying in the wind with spider webs."

"How big are these spiders?" Lizzy wanted to know.

"I have a feeling they're extraordinarily big. I detest spiders," replied Aurora.

"Me, too," Lance chimed in.

"Isn't there another way to get there?" gulped Lizzy.

"You can fly over the forest," declared Soren the elf commander.

"But we won't be able to take all the other soldiers who don't have magic," remarked Lance.

"Have you thought about the dangers of walking through the forest?" Commander Soren asked. "It will be safer for them, and easier for us to transport the captives."

"You're right," Aurora responded. "Charlie, you'll be in charge while we are away. Take care," Aurora says.

Charlie, the troll chief's son replied, "I'll take care of them."

"Thank you, Charlie." Aurora took over the lead of her group.

They only had a day and a half to get the Marauders out of Arth. The elves and the three royals flew over the forest before darkness blanketed the area.

"Ah . . ." everyone stopped and hovered.

"Where is Lizzy?" cried out Aurora.

"She's falling into the forest." Lance cried, pointing to her.

"We're coming, Lizzy!" Aurora shouted.

"Help me!"

"Coming!" shouted Lance.

As Aurora, Lance, and the elves descend into the Arachne Forest, they find themselves caught in silky, sticky webs. Lance exclaimed fearfully as he noticed the gigantic spiders around them.

"Oh my gosh, look at the gigantic spiders! I feel their eyes piercing into me and their teeth ready to take a bite out of me," whimpered Lance.

"I know what you mean, Lance," squealed Aurora.

"Aurora, Lance, hurry, I'm going to be eaten!" yelped Lizzy.

Out of nowhere, the sound of arrows and screams filled the air. The spiders tumbled down from the trees while the elves ignited the webs to set the trio free. Then the elves caught Aurora, Lance, and Lizzy to prevent them from falling and becoming spider food.

"Phew, what a narrow escape," shuddered Aurora.

"You are telling me, I couldn't breathe," whimpered Lizzy, who didn't look well and was not steady on her feet.

Aurora and Lance hugged her. "Are you okay, Lizzy?"

"I think I will be," she said as she threw up. They all felt queasy.

"Spiders can't see, but they can track from the vibrations on the ground and their web," said Lance, knowledgeably.

"Look, here comes Soren with some friends," gulped Lance.

"This is Blaze, the Royal Highness of the centaurs, Your Highnesses," said Soren.

"Thank you, Your Highness, for saving us," each of them said in unison.

"We'd have been food for the spiders if it hadn't been for you," said Lizzy, still wobbly on her feet.

"We don't prevent the natural predator-prey interaction as long as they are only eating birds, squirrels, rabbits, and such," said the King. "Are you okay?" he asked Lizzy.

"Yes, thank you, Your Highness. I will be okay. I'm still queasy, and my heart is thumping so fast," she answered.

The spiders scurried up to the crown of their tree and concealed themselves amid the foliage and boughs.

"The spiders are terrified of my friends here because they are the protectors of the forest," said Soren.

King Blaze and his soldiers escorted them out of the forest.

"Thank you for saving us, Your Highness!" Lance called, waving.

"Yes, Thank you Your Highness for saving me! I hope we meet again under better circumstances," said Lizzy.

"I sure am thankful you were here to help us, Your Highness. Our parents will be very thankful!" Aurora said.

This time all three of them held hands and flew toward Serpent Mountain where the Marauders were mining. They flew over miles and miles of rugged land and mountains.

"Wow, that waterfall is so beautiful and endless," Lizzy exclaimed, feeling a little better. Lance and Aurora agreed.

As the sun set, they caught sight of the Serpent Mountains against the red and orange background—a range that resembled a slithering snake. After a quick stop by Angel Falls Lake, they set up camp, enjoyed a brief meal, and retired to their tents for the night.

"Lizzy, are you sure you're, okay? What happened to you?" asked Aurora.

"Yes, Lizzy, how did you end up falling?" asked Lance.

Lizzy recounted her terrifying experience flying over Arachne Forest. The webs blowing in the wind were a frightening sight, and the thought of spiders made her heart race. She hyperventilated and suddenly felt herself falling rapidly. This was undoubtedly the most scared she had been.

"I know what you're saying," said Lance. "I had to focus on getting to the other side of the forest. But when you fell, and Aurora and I fell, I didn't think we would survive the spiders. My stomach was churning and in knots, and my head throbbed. I'm so glad you're okay, Lizzy."

"My heart was thumping too, and my chest was tight when I couldn't get myself out of their web. The silky web was so strong and restrained my hands tightly. I felt so helpless. My head still hurts. I'm so glad we're all okay," said Aurora.

"I'm glad we're all okay!" said Lance. "Group hug!" And the three of them hugged.

Before they turned in, there was a bright light, and Queen Sophia appeared sitting on an overstuffed sofa. The three ran to her and hugged her. They were so glad to see an adult. They sat next to her on the sofa. Lance sat on an ottoman in front of his Grams.

"Grandma, I'm so happy to see you!" exclaimed Lizzy.

"Me too!" said Aurora.

"Me three!" laughed Lance.

"Oh, my darlings, you did so well, and how brave you were crossing the Arachne Forest. I am so proud of you three." The Queen's maid brought them all a cup of hot cocoa and cookies. They all thanked her.

"Mm . . . it is so good to have warm cocoa and chocolate chip cookies. I'm feeling calm already," sighed Lizzy.

"We were terrified today, Grandma. Those spiders were as big as a small dog, with pincer-like teeth," explained Lance.

"And their web was sticky and very strong. It was hard for us to get free from it."

"Yep, and the centaur King Blaze and his army used their arrows to kill the attacking spiders. And the elves set the webs on fire, Grandma," added Aurora.

"You're okay now, children. You did very well. Tomorrow morning, you will face Prince Raju and his army of men. I want you to be as strong as you were today, facing the spiders. Focus on what you are doing. Be specific about your intention when you're facing off with Raju and his army. You will come into some new powers that will help you. Believe in yourself and what you can do. I've informed your grandmother that you're coming. They are keeping her in the shuttle named Explorer I. Wear your amulet and it will give you strength and energy. All the flying you've done will deplete your energy. So, wear your amulet to sleep tonight to be energized. Use your powers wisely against Raju, my dears. I will see you soon." She hugged all three of them and placed a kiss on each of their foreheads. Before they knew it, all three of them were fast asleep, wearing their ruby amulets. In the morning, they wondered if they really saw their Grandmother Sophia.

"Lance, did you see Grandma Sophia last night?" asked Aurora.

"Yes, I thought it was a dream," he replied.

"Me, too, but the hot cocoa was so soothing that I'm not afraid anymore," said Lizzy.

"I know what you mean, Lizzy. I feel like I'm ready to face our Uncle Raju."

"Same here," said Lance.

"What should we call ourselves?" asked Lance laughingly.

"Woo-hoo! It will be so cool to have a superpower name!" shouted Lizzy.

"Wow! That will be positively magnificent," Aurora cried out.

They spent a few minutes brainstorming noisily, all at the same time. Then, there was a huge outburst from Lizzy, "What about the Ruby Warriors?"

"Hey, what's all the hullabaloo?" Charlie asked, surprising them. "I came here to tell you lot that breakfast is ready."

"You're the first to hear this, Charlie," Lizzy called out." We're calling ourselves, the Ruby Warriors."

"What do you think of that?" inquired Aurora.

"Hoo-wha! That sounds downright phenomenal!" responded Charlie. They all high-five and do a whirly up in the air.

"Come on then, Let's go tell everybody your superhero name," said Charlie.

Everyone was sitting down on the luscious green grass, eating their bowl of oatmeal.

"Listen here friends, our Highnesses have a superhero name for themselves. The trio will from now on be called the Ruby Warriors!" bellowed Charlie. Everyone stood up clapping, cheering, and whistling. They thanked them and sat down for breakfast, enjoying a delicious oatmeal breakfast with warm goat's milk.

"Wow, this goat's milk is a little strong, but it's still good," said Lance.

"Uh-huh," Aurora and Lizzy agreed.

"Congratulations young 'uns. Clever coming up with that name," said Soren with a smile. "Are you ready? We must make time."

CHAPTER 6

Enjoying the Power of Flight

"We will make time by flying to Angel Falls. It takes about two hours to get there as the crow flies," explained Soren.

"This is so amazing to have an aerial view of the ground," said Lance.

"Never in a million years would I have thought that I would fly and have magical powers," Lizzy exclaimed, doing a loop-de-loop.

The three of them found confidence and newfound excitement in their powers as they did stunts in the air, laughing with pure joy in their hearts.

"I know, isn't it amazing?" Aurora cried.

"Your Highnesses, see there, that's Angel Falls," said Soren, pointing. "And we land there."

"Wow, it's so beautiful. Look at the beautiful colors," said Aurora, mesmerized.

"It's like different colors of shiny glass flowing down in sheets," remarked Lance.

"Oh Wow! I could stare at its beauty all day long," shouted Aurora, doing a twirl.

They followed Soren as he headed down to the ground to land. They landed on the lush green grass. The surroundings were peaceful with only the gentle sound of cascading water creating a soothing atmosphere. It was a tranquil and calming experience.

"We better eat something to get our energy back up. Flying is stressful on our bodies, and it depletes our energy," instructed Soren.

They all retrieved their snack bars and drinks and found a spot to sit down.

Aurora, Lance, and Lizzy sat under a huge shady willow tree to enjoy their snacks.

"Don't you think flying across Angel Falls will drain us of our energy?" Lance asked.

"That worries me, too. Let's see what Soren has to say," replied Aurora.

Turning to the commander, Lance asked, "Soren, is there another way to cross Angel Falls other than flying?"

"There sure is Lance. There is a secret passage that is very special."

Lizzy asked, "There aren't any dangerous beasts or anything like that—are there?"

"Oh, no Princess Lizzy. You'll be fine in this forest. We also have friends here," assured Soren.

After resting, everyone was ready for their next journey through the Secret Forest.

The members of the Ruby Warriors gathered their backpacks and ensured that they had cleaned up all their trash. They followed Soren through a serene, wooded area to reach the hidden forest. Along the way, they appreciated the peacefulness and the stunning natural beauty that God had created. At last, Soren halted in front of a mountainside covered with overgrown ivy, sturdy woody shrubs, and clusters of deep red roses with sharp thorns.

Soren blew some fairy dust, and the wall of ivy parted. "We have arrived. Hurry and enter before the portal closes," instructed Soren.

CHAPTER 7

The Trek through the Secret Forest

Making it through the forest, they all heard the happy chirping sounds of birds. The Secret Forest was a luscious green forest with a variety of plant species. There were extraordinary species not known to man and fairies flittering around flowers, getting the nectar into a flask. Some of them were curious and flew to Soren.

"Hi, Soren, who are your friends?' asked Rose.

"Hey, Rose, these are the three great-great-great-great-grandchildren of Queen Sophia," announced Soren.

Rose waved her hand, inviting others to meet the descendants of Queen Sophia. Many beings hurried to meet them. There were aliens, trolls, dwarfs, and fairies.

"Wow! Look at that tall yellow alien, Lizzy, he's waving to us," said Lance.

"We better wave back. Look at his oval head, potbelly, overly long stretchy arms, and skinny long legs," cried Lizzy, amazed.

"Not to mention his round black eyes, bubble nose, and round ears. We don't want to be rude, but we must get going to confront Prince Raju," commented Soren.

"Thank you for allowing us through your beautiful forest. Your secret will be safe with us," Aurora said.

They trekked through the forest and saw more tall yellow aliens with round bellies and disproportionate arms and legs, which were way too long. Their ears stuck out. The yellow aliens were dressed in men's or women's clothing. The women were drying their clothes and their children played beside them.

"We're coming to the exit in a few minutes," Soren said.

He blew the fairy dust, and the portal opened. All went through the portal quickly and came upon another wooded area. For the next leg of the journey, they flew to the other side and landed at the base of Mount Gordo where the rebels were. Quickly, they took out their snacks and drinks to refuel. Then they flew up to the mountain and watched the rebels from behind enormous boulders. Soren declared that the sun was setting, and they would launch their attack under the cover of darkness.

"Lance, can you and Lizzy check out where their camp is? Find Explorer I since we know Grams is there," instructed Soren.

"Sure," replied Lance and Lizzy.

"Guys, also remember to be cloaked when you check things out. This is just a scouting mission for now," reminded Aurora.

"I love you guys!" cried Lizzy, hugging Lance, and Aurora.

"Love you, too, guys!" said Aurora.

"Love you more!" said Lance with a cheeky laugh.

"We're headed into battle. How about we take a few minutes of quiet time to pray for our family and their safety and the safety of Arth?" Lance asked. The three of them bowed their heads and asked God to take away the burden of the world from upon their shoulders and deliver Arth to its former glory.

They hugged each other.

"I wish I could tell Mama, Daddy, and even annoying Billy how much I love them," said Lizzy.

"I know what you mean. I've missed my family so much," replied Aurora.

"They know we love them very much. We will win this battle, you guys. We must be positive. Anyone who survives the Arachne Forest is prepared to face Prince Raju," encouraged Lance.

"It's time to go up the mountain. We will fly up to the mountain where we can see what Prince Raju is up to."

CHAPTER 8

Alas, the Arrival at Serpent Mountain

Soren's Elvin warriors are very skilled at climbing the mountain.

"Arg! This is so hard," moaned Lizzy, "I don't know if I will have the strength to climb all the way to the top. Look at the elves go; you'd think they did this every day."

"Let's fly," exclaimed Aurora. "Soren, we're going to fly to the top."

The three held hands and flew to the top of Serpent Mountain. They hid behind enormous boulders and took their binoculars from their backpacks. Each of them hydrated by drinking a whole flask of water.

"I was so thirsty," said Lance.

"Yeah, Gram told us to fuel ourselves, especially after flying," remembered Lizzy.

Aurora reported, "There are about thirty men in total. There are seven guards, and the rest are prisoners. They are moving wheelbarrows full of what must be diamonds, rubies, and obsidian."

"So, what is our plan?" asked Lance.

"I'll take my soldiers and free the prisoners in the mine," replied Soren. "Then I'll have my men accompany the people to the forest below the valley for safety. I'm going to have Charlie take them all back to the Secret Forest."

"Sounds good, Soren. One less thing to worry about," said Lance.

"And the three of us will save our Grandma Shanti and put the guards in the shuttle and put them to sleep," instructed Aurora. "Soren, your men will deliver the rebel guards to their shuttle and put them to sleep. Do you need some Unicorn dust to put them to sleep?"

"No, thanks, the fairy dust I have will also do the same thing," answered Soren.

The three of them high-fived each other. "Good Luck Soren!" all three chimed in.

"Good Luck to you, Your Highnesses!" replied Soren.

"Let's follow those men since they're obviously taking the loot to their space shuttle," said Lance.

The three followed the group quietly, under the cover of their cloaking device. They came to a wooded area, and the men went through it. The trio, hiding behind trees and bushes, followed the group.

"Omg! Look at that. How clever of them to have found a forest with a clearing in the middle of it," Lizzy burst out.

"Ingenious!" exclaimed Lance.

"Gramma Sophia said that Gramma Shanti will be in Explorer I," Aurora reminded them.

"Are we going to take their power out? Their camp is lit so brightly!" complained Lizzy.

"We'll have to work with the lights on. They, too, are magical beings who can use magic to bring the lights back on," replied Lance.

"We'll have to take care of the rebel guards watching the shuttle. The three of us will use our invisibility to put them to sleep and hide them behind those barrels."

"That sounds like a plan, Aurora!" said Lizzy, high-fiving Aurora, and Lance.

"Yep!" said Lance.

CHAPTER 9

Saving Grandma Shanti and Their Friends

The three of them were getting closer and closer to the shuttles. They looked around the shuttle area.

"Three men are watching each of the shuttles," noticed Lizzie.

"So, we blow the Unicorn's dust at them?" Aurora asked.

"Yes, according to the book we had to read," answered Lance, "they will sleep for about eight to ten hours."

"We'll go cloaked into their camp and get Grandma Shanti out first," suggested Lizzie. "She can be helpful to us."

"Ok, let's go then," Lanced said, nodding.

Under the cover of invisibility, they got on Explorer I. Three techs were watching their security cameras.

Lizzy blew the Unicorn dust, "Whoo . . ."

All three techs fell, and the heroes put them in a comfortable position in their seats.

They slowly walked, still invisible, to the very back. "There's a guard standing in front of the cabin door," Lance whispered. Pointing to the guard and then himself, he swiftly took the guard out. "Whoo . . .." He blew, and the tall, hefty guard fell.

Aurora and Lizzie quickly entered the cabin at the back of the shuttle, and there were no guards.

"I knew you were close. My dears, we must hasten. They have been loading their loot," exclaimed Grandma Shanti.

"You're the one we saw at the gem store!" gasped Lizzy.

They all hugged their grandma.

"Grandma, stay here till we get the guards outside," said Lance boldly. The Ruby Warriors cloaked themselves to put the guards outside to sleep.

"I'll levitate the guards and send them into the shuttle, and Grandma can help them into their seats and their safety belts?" Lance asked.

"Of course, Lance, I can do that," said Grandma.

"All right guys, we have to do this at the same time," said Lance, taking a deep breath. Each of them stood in front of their enemy, blew the Unicorn's dust, and they fell asleep. They immediately levitated them and sent them to the shuttle.

"Grandma Shanti, come on, we must go. Can you turn invisible?" asked Aurora.

"Of course, my darlings!" said Grandma.

Lance suggested that the goal be to reach the other shuttle, and he asked Grandma to repeat the actions she took in Explorer I.

"I can do that, Lance," Grandma replied.

As soon as they entered Explorer IV, they heard chatter. Grandma walked back in her invisible self to wait in the back of the shuttle.

"There are four of them!" Lizzy said softly.

"It'll be okay," assured Lance, "I'll take two of them, Lizzy."

"Okay, are you ready?" asked Aurora.

"Yep!" responded Lizzy.

"Yep!" responded Lance.

"Whooo . . ." they both blew the Unicorn's dust.

They sent the sleeping guards to the back row of the cabin, and Grandma set them in their seats and seat belted them.

"Go along, my darlings, and do what you do best. I will finish here as you send them in," said Grandma Shanti.

"There are three of them outside. Are we ready?" Lance asked.

"Yeah!" said Lizzy.

"Yep!" said Aurora.

"Whooo . . ." They all blew the Unicorn's dust. After getting the three guards to sleep, they sent them into the cabin of the shuttle for Grandma to seat and belt them in. Once they were all in the cabin, they made sure all lights were off. They all retreated to the wooded area to meet Soren; the four of them held hands to teleport.

"I'm happy to see you all. Did you see Prince Raju? "Asked Soren.

"No, we didn't," answered Aurora.

"How did it go with your team?" asked Lance.

"We freed the elves and took away the chains that bound their powers. So, we had plenty of firepower. Some of them without powers were sent back with Charlie and his team to the valley. I told them if we don't come back in a day and a half to head back to the villages," Soren replied.

"Don't worry, Soren, we will make it back. Positive thoughts only people," Lizzy said, grinning.

"Okay, let's head out to find Prince Raju. Does anyone know where he might be?" Aurora queried.

"I do Your Highness!" A hand raised up high.

"Hi! What's your name?" asked Aurora with a smile.

"I am Enos, and I was the one who served Prince Raju his meals and drinks," he answered, bowing.

"So, tell us, Enos, where he is hiding?" asked Lance, shaking Enos's hand.

"Well, Prince Raju is hiding in a cave. He has three caves he hides in. He does not trust anyone. I even must taste his food," replied Enos.

"Can you take us to these caves?" asked Lizzy.

"I sure can, Your Highnesses."

"Enos, let's drop the Highnesses part for now, okay?" remarked Lance.

Lizzy and Aurora nodded in agreement.

The three Ruby Warriors and Soren came together to strategize and talk about what to do next. "It might be easier to draw him out. Looks like he's afraid of the Ruby Warriors or he wouldn't be hiding," said Soren.

"Okay, once we find where he is, we will draw him out."

"I know how to get him out!" shouted Lizzy, "I will go into his cave with a couple of your soldiers, Soren, and we will start fires in it to draw him out."

"Hey, that sounds like a great idea, Lizzy," said Lance, "and then we'll get together and try to get the chains that bind him around his waist, or hands."

"Yep, a brilliant plan," Soren agreed enthusiastically, "Once the chains get him, they will clamp on tightly so he can't use magic."

"Okay guys, Lizzy's plan is great. We must get him into the space shuttle by noon today. It is 4:30 a.m. now so we need to go," cautioned Aurora.

"Everyone—take fifteen minutes to hydrate and eat a snack," said Soren seriously. "We go against Prince Raju today."

The group flew and landed in the wooded area by the first cave Monahan took them. Soren, Lizzy, and Monahan go in.

CHAPTER 10

Hunting Prince Raju

"Prince Raju is not here, but we'll still burn down his hideout so he can't use it again," said Lizzy.

"Yep, let's do it," Soren agreed.

Monahan went out and made an X with his arms to signal to the others that Raju wasn't there.

As soon as Soren and Lizzy came out, smoke billowed from the cave. They took off again to his second hideout. This one was in a wooded area close to a stream.

Lizzy, Soren, and Monahan went inside the cave quietly, wearing their invisible shields. They looked everywhere, but there was no Prince Raju.

Hm . . . He seems to like his creature comforts, I see. Lizzy thought.

Again, they set the place on fire. This time, they left a few elves so the fire would not get out of control.

Going to the third cave, they hovered over it cautiously and quietly to see if Prince Raju was by the stream or in the woods.

"Okay, we form a kinda circle from the entrance of the cave. Do exactly what we talked about," said Lance.

They all nodded and got ready to make their attack.

"I will go in first, Your Highness, then Monahan, and you follow. Okay?" said Soren.

"Okay," Lizzy agreed, nodding her head.

Oh wow, I can hardly believe the time has come. Thought Lizzy.

She then followed Monahan. She could hear swords striking against one another. Prince Raju was here.

Lizzy cloaked herself and "Whoo . . ." blew the Unicorn's dust.

"Ah . . . Choo," sneezed Prince Raju, but nothing happened.

Lizzy and Charlie started the fires in the back of the cave.

"Soren, Soren, get out now! Hurry Soren," shouted Lizzy.

Lizzy hurried to join Lance and Aurora.

"Soren, please come out," pled Aurora.

At the entrance, Soren came out holding his side, blood blooming down his sleeve. A couple of elves picked Soren up and escaped with him by using their invisibility.

"He's coming out, but he is afraid. He knows that the Ruby Warriors are here and is afraid that the prophecy will come true," said Lance.

"Lance, you have your powers of telepathy," whispered Aurora.

When Prince Raju came out, Aurora's senses heightened, and she projected a hologram of them surrounding Prince Raju. They quickly switched places so that Prince Raju wouldn't know where they were.

"Lay down your weapon, Uncle Raju," warned Lizzy in an icy voice.

"Aah, my brother has told you who I am. Good for him. You know, children, he has missed seeing all of you," Prince Raju said, smiling cunningly.

"We're not children, Uncle Raju. Agree to come with us willingly and to wear the bracelets," ordered Lance confidently.

"No way! I like my freedom too much, and I will rule Arth one day, and then I will conquer your Earth!" cried Prince Raju, throwing fireballs.

"You're scared, Uncle, and I can feel your body trembling. You know the prophesy well and know that the Ruby Warriors can defeat you," taunted Lance.

"You're lying. I will defeat you." Raju threw balls of fire haphazardly and made himself invisible.

"My arrow will find you, Uncle!" Lance shouted.

The elves got ready to throw the binding chains when the arrow hits him. Lance shot the arrow to wound Prince Raju in his right shoulder. The arrow found its mark and so did the elves. As soon as the arrow hit, Prince Raju wasn't invisible anymore; so, they threw the chains, immediately binding Prince Raju's power. They used stainless-steel handcuffs, which work just as well as chains.

"How does it feel, Uncle, to be caged?" asked Aurora.

"HUH!" Prince Raju responded and turned away.

"Take him out of there, soldier! Thank you," commanded Lizzy.

"Hey, hey! What do you want to do with me?" asked Prince Raju worriedly.

"Unlike you, Uncle, I want to heal your wounds before we send you back," Lizzy answered, laying her hand over his blood-soaked shirt. His wound healed at once. "Is there any other place you're hurt that we can't, see?" she asked.

"Well, I think I have broken some ribs—can't tell how many."

"Okay, lay still," Lizzy ordered, putting her hand over the shirt. She spread her palm over the ribcage and heard Prince Raju taking a deep breath.

"Okay, Uncle, you're all fixed." Turning to the others, she said, "You may put him back and take him immediately to Explorer IV. Happy trails Uncle Raju."

"Thank you, Lizzy! I didn't expect you to be so kind," said the prince.

"You're welcome. If you could have only shown kindness to the people of Arth and negotiated for supplies, we wouldn't be here today."

"As far as I know, all individuals have boarded both shuttles," Monahan reported to the Ruby Warriors.

"We're ready to send them off to space," Lance announced.

"Okay then, we'll teleport them out of here using a portal," said Aurora.

"Okay guys let's do it," Lizzy ordered.

The three of them swiped their right hands counterclockwise. "Swoosh" a swirling portal opened and pulled both shuttles in.

"Goodbye," each of them said, waving happily.

They flew down to the valley, and everyone at camp clapped and whistled.

"How is Soren?" asked Lizzy.

"He's not doing so well," Grandma Shanti replied.

"Take me to him."

"Hi, Soren, I'm here to make you feel better. After I'm done, you won't know what hit you," said Lizzy.

"What happened to Prince Raju?"

"We captured him, put them all to sleep, and sent them back to Mars where they will be put away for a very long time," she answered as she laid her palm on his sides and then on his arm. She touched his forehead, and it was hot, so she placed her palm on his forehead. He was feeling better already.

"Any other place hurting you?"

"No, everything is good, Your Highness!" Soren jumped out of bed and twirled her around. Everyone burst out laughing.

"Everyone, tomorrow we head home," Soren announced.

"Grandpa's going to be happy to see you, Grams," Lizzy said, smiling.

"I'm eager to see your Grandpa, too."

The Ruby Warriors hug each other tightly. "I'll be seeing Mom and Dad soon," said Aurora. "I've even missed Little Jimmy being a pest."

"I have missed Mom and Dad's hugs so much. I realized I need to listen to my younger sister a little more. I have been a terrible older sister to her. The first thing I'm going to do is take Annie to the park," announced Lizzy.

"Oh my gosh, I have positively gone crazy not knowing if we would see them again. I'm going to give them a tight hug and tell them I love them," said Lance. "I've missed them so much. I'm also going to be nicer to the twins and watch them more when Mom asks."